MUST
DO
BETTER

Tales of a Teaching Assistant

Michelle Monan

Grosvenor House
Publishing Limited

This book is published by
Grosvenor House Publishing Ltd
Link House
140 The Broadway, Tolworth, Surrey, KT6 7HT.
www.grosvenorhousepublishing.co.uk

A CIP record for this book
is available from the British Library

ISBN 978-1-80381-366-0

Find me on Facebook - 'Children's Author Michelle Monan'

ACKNOWLEDGEMENTS

I would like to thank Grosvenor House Publishing for accepting my manuscript and turning it into a book. They have been patient and honest and have offered much needed advice.

Ruairi Cassidy designed the book cover which is exactly how I had imagined it would be. Thank you for your time and creativity.

Thank you to my family who have put up with me throughout my time of working in these schools and nurseries. They've wiped my tears, given me big hugs and always been there for me. I couldn't have got through this period without their support and kind and loving words and actions.

INTRODUCTION

When I first thought of putting all my school and nursery experiences on paper I was filled with positivity and humorous tales with all the funny things that children have said over the years, but I'm conscious that it hasn't turned out like that.

I kept a diary of all the settings I've been to which has helped jog my memory, but most of my memories are not good ones, apart from the odd one or two. I will be first to say this is a fairly negative account of my role as a Teaching Assistant.

I've dipped in and out of writing this when I'm in all sorts of moods, but it always takes a dark turn. There are enjoyable moments, but teaching is an extremely challenging role.

There are more and more adverts on both the radio and TV for teachers and they always make it sound like it's so rewarding, which it can be, but it can also be incredibly soul destroying and depressing. There is currently a teacher crisis and perhaps you'll see why after reading my account.

This is my story of real places, real people and real events. Some are shocking, sickening and concerning, while others are uplifting and joyful. No names have been mentioned of children, staff, schools, nurseries or agencies, it has all been written with confidentiality at the foremost.

It has been incredibly cathartic and therapeutic writing this book. I had so many memories and thoughts running around in my head that they needed to come out somehow so I thought it best to put them in a book rather than take it out on my family with ranting and raving and crying and I now feel so much better for it. I would thoroughly recommend it to anyone in a job with stories to tell. It has come as an enormous release and relief to write it all down.

Every job comes with its difficulties, but being a Teaching Assistant is a far cry from what people may think who don't work in that environment. We certainly don't spend our days playing with children and making things out of crepe paper and glue. It isn't my intention to put people off going into this industry, but I just want it to be known what goes on, from my own experience.

In between all the stories I've told in this book I have worked with many SEN children who I have not written about. This is due to their needs and conditions of which they have no control and I didn't think it would be fair to comment on my experiences with them. I have mainly focussed on those with behaviour issues who can control themselves, but often choose to do so in a negative way, making our job very difficult.

I came into this industry because I wanted to make a difference, but it's been extremely challenging and a period of my life that I'll never forget. I have met and worked with countless children during my time as a TA and many of them have been delightful, but it seems to be the ones that aren't so delightful that I've remembered!

I can't begin to imagine what it must be like living with some of the children I've worked with. I often wonder if they behave at home as they do at school, if their behaviour is better or worse with their parents than it is with their teachers. I'd love to be a fly on the wall in some of their homes just to see.

CHAPTER 1

Inever knew what I wanted to do for a job when I was young. I wasn't one of those people who had a career in mind or a vocation to aim for. I don't regret any of the jobs I have done as I think they've made me who I am. I particularly enjoyed my time when I was young working in pubs, bars and restaurants as it was a great experience to work with the general public and my God that's a whole other story!

When you're young and have only really been around your own family and friends, it's a complete eye opener to see how other people behave and carry on especially in the hospitality industry with a lot of customers treating staff like slaves, clicking their fingers and not a please or thank you to be heard. Nothing's changed since then. I still hear people ordering drinks with no manners and it rattles me. Manners don't cost anything and make the world a nicer place.

I had an office job during the day for several years and met girls who have become lifelong friends and we see each other regularly, four decades on, so I consider that job one of my best for that reason.

When I was 25 I had my first child and my second at 31, both boys. I had no plans to have any more, but when the youngest was 3 years old and had started nursery I realised how much I missed them both during the day so had a rethink of my future. It was then I thought about working in a nursery school myself to gain experience and to still be around children.

I applied for a job at a local school and took to it like a duck to water. It was so much fun and the days flew by as we were all kept busy and the children were a joy to work with. This was a 9am to 3pm setting which fitted in perfectly with the rest of my life. I couldn't have been happier.

I must have been there for about 6 months and had already started my NVQ3 at college, when it was brought to my attention that a setting, not too far away, was up for sale. This wasn't something I had ever considered, not for a moment, but I kind of knew I wanted to do something other than just work in a nursery for years to come so I looked into it and, after being interviewed several times by different childcare authorities, I became the owner of my own setting. Luckily the staff who aready worked there stayed on and I drew from their experiences which I will be forever grateful.

After just one year of owning this one and gaining a fantastic reputation, to the point we had a very long waiting list, I was approached by Ofsted following an 'Good' inspection, that another setting was for sale and would I be interested in purchasing it. This offer in itself was testiment to how I was managing my nursery and within a year I was the owner of two settings.

I met two lovely ladies at college who were on the same course as me and they became my invaluable staff at the second nursey. They were older than me and already had years of experience so I learnt a lot from both of them.

I was equally as lucky with my staffing at this nursery as they all stayed on and we all worked well as a team. There was never any falling out or even many disagreements, which I came to find out in the future, happens all the time, so I think myself very lucky with my ladies in both places.

I could probably count on less than two hands, over a 10 year period, how many staff left and how many I had to employ. Most left only because they were pregnant or leaving the country or just wanted a complete change of job.

I like to think I was a nice boss who was approachable, friendly and would take on board any suggestions or advice that my staff had. I also felt incredibly proud that both settings had fantastic reputations, always had long waiting lists and our Ofsted inspections were a credit to how we ran the nurseries throughout my time as owner.

After 10 years of doing this I came to the difficult decision that it was time for me to do something else. As much as I had enjoyed my role it was becoming like Groundhog Day and I had had enough. More and more children with Special Needs were coming through and so many children with behaviour issues, which I found more difficult to cope with.

I was also finding Child Protection Case Conferences very difficult to attend as they are an emotional ordeal and I was taking it all home with me mentally, which wasn't good for me or my poor family. There are some details in these meetings which you can't unhear and they stay with you.

Unbeknown to me at the time I had entered into my menopause, which now explains why I was feeling the way I was (losing my patience easily, aggrevated by small things, everyone starting to get on my nerves, and all the other emotions that go with this horrid time in a woman's life). It took me a year to sell them both. I did feel bad leaving the girls with new owners, but this was something I needed to do for myself.

CHAPTER 2

I felt a huge weight off my shoulders once both sales had gone through and suddenly I had time on my hands. Even though we had all the school holidays, as an owner it never stopped. There was always something to be done whether it was paperwork or sorting the settings out, so to suddenly not have that after 10 years was an odd feeling.

Although it did feel very strange at first, it didn't take long for me to enjoy my free time. I had decided to give myself a year to have a complete break from work and just do what I wanted when I wanted.

After about 4 months of this I realised there's only so much housework and gardening you can do. My friends were all working, my husband and eldest son were working and my youngest was at school.

I would often go all day without talking to anyone apart from the birds, squirrels, mice and plants in my garden, but of course none of those can talk back so that was a one way form of communication.

I actually reached a point of looking forward to getting a nuisance call just so I could have a conversation. "No I haven't been in an accident lately" and "No I don't want a conservatory", but I dragged it out just to talk to somebody, I mean - how bad/sad is that?

If I didn't get any calls during the day and I was indoors because of bad weather it wouldn't be until my family started coming home that I would finally speak and my voice would be wobbly and croaky where it hadn't been used all day. I knew this wasn't good. I was bored and needed to do something, for my sanity as much as anything else.

I enjoyed the summertime then looked for work, doing something completely different, away from children. I went into research for 4 years and recruitement for just over a year, but actually found adults harder work than children!

In one of those jobs I often became fearful for my own safety and when I now drive near any of the areas I worked in then, I can feel myself getting very anxious at the thought of it.

Thinking about it now, I'm surprised I did it for as long as I did, but it was a job I was good at and I quickly became a tutor to new staff in guiding them through what was required to make people want us to come into their homes and interview them.

I live in an affluent area in the south of England and consider myself very lucky with what I have. This job was mainly within a 30 mile radius, although most of it was carried out within about 7 miles, but some of the homes I visited were unbelievable, and not in a good way. I had to knock on doors and be invited in to undertake the research, but there were many occasions when I really didn't want to go in.

I know you shouldn't judge a book by it's cover, but I found there are a lot of people at home during the day that have a serial killer look about them (more Fred West than Ted Bundy) and I was not going to enter their homes for the sake of research.

If I didn't like what I saw or felt uncomfortable I would make an appointment so I didn't have to go inside, and then follow it up with some excuse not to return. This happened more times than I care to remember.

On the other end of the scale though I did get to visit some astonishing homes and wonderful people, talk about how the other half live. Again, this job is another story in itself with many memories I would rather forget.

At the back of my mind, in the last year or so of this job, I had been thinking what a waste of time all my childcare training was. When you work with children there are always courses that you have to take, whether they are refresher courses or new ones, and I had taken so many over the years. Was I happier working with children than adults? Yes I think I was.

I looked online for what kind of work I could do. I knew I didn't really want to work in a nursery anymore. I was getting older and I felt I wanted to support primary school age children.

I thought about working in a school on a permanent basis, but then I came across an agency that covered everything from nursery to college. This was ideal, I thought. I registered with them, having gone to their offices to meet them and introduce myself. They were very impressed with my CV and experience and were keen to take me on. All I had to do now was wait for the work to come rolling in.

CHAPTER 3

I didn't have to wait long. I was contacted almost immediately with a job, but it was in a full day care setting, despite me having said to this agency that I would rather not take a step back and work with pre-school children! They told me it was only to help out while a member of staff was on holiday and, because of my background, I was the best on their books for this role.

I went with a positive mind and my usual big smiley face. I noticed that I was the only one smiling when I got there. All the staff looked incredibly miserable and this made me feel rather uncomfortable. The manager gave me a brief tour and, as it was only a small setting, this didn't take long. It had an unsettling feel about it, but I didn't know why.

One little boy came bounding up to me like I was a long lost friend and wrapped his arms around my legs hugging me tight. This was a lovely first impression of the children and I got stuck into what was a very long day, starting at 8am and not finishing until 6pm. These were hours I had not been used to, ever. Made worse by the fact that there were no coffee breaks and lunch was strictly one hour, starting at 11.30am, so you can imagine what a long afternoon it was.

I bonded with the children and actually found it quite refreshing just being able to play with them, teach them and support them rather than having to worry about planning, policies, profiles etc etc. The staff were all very young and all seemed so unhappy.

One girl told me that working in a nursery wasn't what she had imagined it would be and that she was already looking to leave and do something completely different. She had only worked at this setting for a few months since completing her training and "hated it".

I couldn't help but notice another member of staff who was sitting down resting her back against a wall, playing with the toys but not the children, and just seemed in another world. I had been there for 3 hours and was all over the place, making sure children were safe and playing together nicely, even changing nappies, then realised that this girl hadn't moved at all! She threw out lots of orders to other staff members, but stayed routed all that time. I'm thinking that this must be unusual surely? Unhappy, lazy staff! It wasn't a good start to my new agency work.

I was asked to return to this setting for the rest of the week. They had given me good feedback to the agency and wanted me to stay on - probably because I was the only one who was doing any work there. I hadn't been used to being surrounded by people who just didn't want to be where they were. Why were they doing it if they were so unhappy?

I seemed to be the only one there that engaged with the children. I had hoped that my first day was maybe just a one off and that they would all be more cheery later in the week, but it stayed the same. I carried on working at this day care for two months and found myself getting very low in my mood, so different to how I had started off. This had to be because of the people around me, they were bringing me down.

Some of the staff barely opened their mouths when they spoke, like it was an effort to talk, and walked around like they had all the worries of the world on their shoulders. The only time they were chatty was in the staffroom at lunch time, but even then, they were all so bitchy towards each other.

Every time anyone left the room they would talk about them in an awful way. I could feel my toes curling at some of the language they were using and the way they were talking about their colleagues.

I just kept quiet and ate my lunch, dreading what they would say about me when I left the room! It got so bad I ended up having my lunch in my car and going for a walk around the area when it wasn't raining.

I asked the agency a few times if there was anything else available, but my only option was either there or another full day care centre which was miles away. The person I was covering who was off sick never came back and they were having a staff shortage crisis.

Over the weekend I looked online again to see if there was a different agency, one that dealt mainly with schools and, after reading very good reviews about one in particular, I registered with them. I visited them in their offices for my interview and felt uplifted just by doing this knowing that I would finally be working in a school with primary age children.

CHAPTER 4

Itook a few weeks off to enjoy what was left of the school holidays and was geared up to work in a local school. I had been offered to work in Year 2 as a general TA (Teaching Assistant) and got there early to show goodwill and incase I had to read policies, sign paperwork or just go through the daily timetable. Everyone there was so lovely. The ladies in the office couldn't have been friendlier and the Head Teacher made a point of coming to find me to introduce herself.

I was shown around this small school and taken to Year 2, but then a teacher came rushing in the room all flustered and said that I was now needed in the nursery department due to a staff shortage and that Year 2 would have to manage without a TA for that day.

I could feel myself deflate, but tried to think positive. It couldn't be any worse than my experience of that first day care centre and I now had my foot in the door of a local school.

As this appeared to be a last minute decision, I was only in the nursery room for about 2 minutes before the children started arriving so I had no idea if any of them needed extra support for SEN (Special Educational Needs), ESL (English as a second language), behaviour issues or anything else that I should have been informed about before the doors opened.

The lady in charge seemed really nice and I could see she was clearly stressed as I was not the only Supply TA, there was another lady, from the same agency, who was also there for her first day. So two people new to the nursery and one relatively new member of staff with only the manager to explain everything while also running the day. It was a case of finding where things were for ourselves and going with the flow.

As I had had lots of experience with children over the years I could tell at a glance those that had needs so made a beeline towards them individually to meet them and support them. Luckily it wasn't a particularly busy nursery.

It was the first day back of a new term so some of them were new and upset, while those who had been there before seemed happy to be back and play with familiar toys and their friends that they hadn't seen since last term.

One little boy was inconsolable when his mum left. There was as much snot as tears and in no time he was a big, wet, soggy mess who I had taken to comfort, so I too was a soggy mess with my top needing a wash before the day had even really begun!

There may have only been a few children, 12 if I recall, but tears were infectious and before long more than half of them were crying their eyes out and clawing at the door. I felt for them I really did, but at the same time I was thinking "Oh my God".

I had woken up thinking I was going to be working in a classroom with a teacher leading the class and I would be helping as a TA, but this was very different to my vision.

The other new TA was feeling the same way. Even though we didn't know each other at all, I could tell from the way she was looking that she wasn't happy with this situation. At least she knew she was going to be in a nursery, but wasn't expecting so many tears and upset. It was manic.

Inbetween comforting those who were upset I was asked to change a nappy. This agency had stated that we are not required to do that and can refuse, but who else was going to do it? The manager couldn't leave the main room and that only left me and the other TA's who had occupied themselves.

I wouldn't have minded too much, but this particular nappy was like nothing I'd ever seen, even with hundreds of changes of my own children over the years, let alone all the children that came through my nurseries.

Fortunately I made sure I had everything to hand - wipes, nappy bags, clean nappy and the bin and I had put rubber gloves on before I undertook this operation. I could smell that this was more than just a wee, but my goodness me, the nappy was not only full of the most foul poo, it was up the poor child's back and in all his creases.

It looked to me as though this had been there a while, possibly all night, meaning he came to nursery in this state, no wonder he was one of the ones who was crying.

I quickly called to the manager before cleaning him up so that she could see the state of this child. I don't know how many wipes I went through to clean him up, really he needed a bath - he was inexusably dirty! Added to this he was wriggling around like a snake round a tree which made my job all the more difficult.

He was noticeably, and rightly so, uncomfortable. The smell was so bad it was going down my throat and making me gag. He had no change of clothes in his bag so I had to put spare nursery clothes on him, which should be washed and returned by the parent, but they never came back.

This was a regular occurance with this child I soon discovered after I returned for the rest of the week and the next two weeks after that. This was my first experience of such a neglected child. He wore the same clothes all week and smelt so bad all the time it was difficult to get too close to him.

I felt like I wanted to take him home, give him a nice warm, bubbly bath, dress him in snug clothes and cuddle him forever. He was an adorable child who just needed to be loved. I never did get the chance to work in a classroom at this school in that 3 week period.

CHAPTER 5

As I was now with two agencies, it was a case of waiting for my phone to ring or an email to arrive to see what I was offered and, as I never knew if both were going to contact me with a choice, I tended to take whatever was offered by the first one that I heard from, which tended to be an early morning phone call.

Over the weekend I couldn't help but keep thinking about that poor neglected boy at that school, so needed to go elsewhere to clear my mind and focus on a new group of children.

For one day I was sent to another Day Nursery, but just for the afternoon. This was a converted big old house with a lovely garden so I was looking forward to having a look around (because I'm quite nosey) as well as working in a different setting.

It was split into 3 floors with the youngest on the top, 6 to 18 months, then 18 months to 3 years on the middle floor and 3 to 4 years on the bottom floor. The stairs were steep and especially narrow leading to the top floor. Of course this would be ok for a house, but as a nursery it was made very difficult when it came to outdoor play as staff had to carry the children down 3 flights of stairs.

I was on the top floor with the youngest group. I made sure I very carefully carried one child at a time so that I could hold onto the stair rail for safety, but the regular staff were carrying one child in each arm so not able to hold onto anything. This made me really worried and scared.

I couldn't begin to imagine the outcome if any of them had lost their footing and fallen! Some of the older children in this group walked down by themselves, with an adult next to them holding other children. I wondered what would happen if the fire alarm went off as there would be panic as well as risk. This was an accident waiting to happen!

As well as that there was generally a lot of going up and down the stairs, taking them to the toilet (including nappy changing) which were only on the middle and lower floors and getting the food from the kitchen which seemed to be ongoing. As soon as lunch was over preparation was being done for their afternoon snack and then tea for those who were still there at 5pm, which was most of them.

I felt like I hadn't interacted much at all with the children at this setting, it was all hands on with clearing up, toilet and nappies and food. I was definitely more of a skivvy and a cleaner than a TA as none of the other staff seemed bothered about cleaning up or even putting things away.

I was run ragged and wondered what it was like when I wasn't there. Do they rely on agency staff to do all the tidying all the time? It definitely came across that way as none of the regular staff had any intention of doing anything other than sitting around.

I suppose to be fair to them they did have their planning, assessments and profiles to do, but they were certainly making the most of me being there to drag that out. I was so glad when it came to 6pm and my half day was over. I had actually started to grind my teeth from anxiety, especially about the stairs!

A phone call at 6.30am took me to another Day Nursery. I feel like I can't refuse incase nothing else comes in. This was a relatively local setting, but an absolute devil to get to, with heavy traffic on the morning commute not helping. Despite leaving in plenty of time to get there I was 20 minutes late which was not a good start.

This was all in one big hall where there were 45 children of all ages and a lot of them crying when I arrived (not *because* I had arrived!). At least there were no stairs to battle, but what a racket. Each sound echoed because of the size of the hall and you can imagine what 45 children sound like, even when they're just playing and not crying. It was intense.

There was a little group of children who, straight away, I felt I needed to keep an eye on as there was a lot of pushing and shoving and arguing over toys. None of them even seemed to actually play with any toys, they were all just picking things up and then throwing them, quite forcefully, on the floor.

This setting had lots of toys and equipment and it seemed like they were all out, it was too much I felt. The children hadn't been taught to put anything away when it was tidy up time and the room looked like a bomb had hit it when they were gathered on two separate mats for story time.

It was up to me and another TA to tidy everything away even though neither of us knew where anything went. We were trying to do this as quietly as possible because the children were listening to a story, but that in itself was an impossibility as two staff members were reading two different stories to two groups of children in this echoey hall. It was a joke.

I don't know if it's because I've run nurseries of my own that I feel things have changed so much for the worse or whether it's just this is how it is nowadays. Whatever it is I'm just getting on with the job in hand and keeping my head down, but it's so hard to bite my tongue when obvious things could be changed for the better. Nobody seems to have any common sense.

For the rest of the week I was back at the one and only school I've been to so far, but this time knowing I was going to be in the nursery. I felt quite confident when I arrived having been there before as I knew what to expect. I was looking forward to seeing the little neglected boy as I had been worried about him and I had hoped that maybe my experience with him may have been a blip, but the family had moved out of the area, which to me made this situation even more worrying. Alarm bells were definitely ringing! I hope he'll be ok wherever he is.

CHAPTER 6

Finally, I got an early morning call to go to a school and work in Year 3. I leapt out of bed with a spring in my step. It was an easy drive with plenty of parking, which is always a good start. I was slightly apprehensive that things might change, but they didn't.

I was working in a classroom with primary children. They were very polite and well mannered and it set me up to thinking I had made the right decision, it had just taken a little while to get to this point.

[The last time I was in a primary school classroom was when I was a child myself so we're talking 50 years ago (crikey, writing that down seems so much longer ago than just saying it!). My earliest memories of school are how the lessons used to seem so long and we had a lot of time to do our work. I was always writing or drawing something.

Now that I'm familiar with a lot of different conditions I can definitely look back and realise that lots of the children I was at school with had needs, we just didn't know about them at that time. I especially remember a boy who used to find food to eat out of the bins and he would wear the same school uniform for weeks, which let off a nasty stale smell. None of us realised that he was a 'neglected child' we just thought he was dirty and disgusting.

The children who we assumed were 'thick' or 'naughty' almost certainly had ADHD or Autism or similar. If only those conditions were known about then so many children could have had the support that there is now. Nobody can even so much as shout or fidget these days without giving it a name or a condition.

On a lighter side, I also remember two of the teachers in particular wearing very short skirts all the time. It was the early 70's and this was the fashion, but I remember those legs, even all these years later. I may have only been very young, but I clearly remember thinking and hoping that all women must have legs like that and that's what I would look like when I grow up...... WRONG!]

My first observation at this school was how rushed everything was. As I was new to this I had no idea how schools operated, but it was like the children had very little time to actually do any work once the teaching was over.

The first lesson was Maths and it took 40 minutes for the teacher to explain what was expected of them which only left 20 minutes for them to do the work themselves before playtime. The teacher spoke really quickly and even I couldn't understand a lot of what she was saying.

When work began so many of them had their hands up for help that it was impossible to assist them all between just me and the class teacher. I found the same happened for the next lesson, English, and again after lunch for the two remaining lessons.

I asked in the staffroom if this was normal and they all said that there was so much to get through that this was the only way. They didn't like having to rush, but felt there was no choice because of having to follow the curriculum.

I must say my head was spinning by the end of the day with the whirlwind of it all, but I did find myself at this school for a full month as I was only offered nursery work otherwise. I couldn't fault the children, infact I bonded quite quickly with a lot of them and looked forward to going in and supporting them.

The only struggle I had was with some of their names as the majority were from different countries and I didn't want to mispronounce them, but other than that I enjoyed my time at this school, if only the pace had been a bit slower.

CHAPTER 7

For my sins I returned to the nursery in the big hall and it was exactly as I had remembered, loud and unorganised. I never went back after today as it was just too much. The children didn't seem to be learning anything other than how to make a mess and there were no consequences for any bad behaviour - and there was alot of that.

Neither were they rewarded or even praised for anything positive that they did. I seemed to be the only one who gave any kind of emotion for their actions and I could feel I was being talked about. I didn't like it and I was worried how these children would cope when they go to school when they weren't being encouraged to do anything.

It didn't help with the actions of the staff either though. Several times I saw them throw objects across the room to each other instead of passing them. For the sake of a few steps they were sending completely the wrong signals to the children.

They would also shout a lot, but then it was very difficult to hear in that room. Children pick up on things we do so we should always be very careful what we do and say and to set a good example to them, that's just common sense.

Back to the first school I visited, but this time I was in Year 2 and not the nursery, oh joy! Again the teaching was quite rushed, maybe not as much as the other school, but even so, there wasn't a lot of time for the children to complete their work after the teaching part of the lesson.

Some children began to get upset as they hadn't finished their work when it was amost playtime, while others dropped everything to go out to play and didn't seem at all bothered that they hadn't finished. Maybe this is how it is everywhere now?

I was in the class with an SEN Supply who was working on a 1-2-1 with a little girl who was mildly autistic. I rather liked the idea of working this way rather than being a general TA so I undertook more courses for Special Needs training over a period of time so that I too could work on a 1-2-1

I also found that staffroom gossip was mainly moaning from TA's about how much they were expected to do. I'm not a lazy person, far from it actually, but it doesn't bode well to hear nothing but complaints from people who have been TA's for years in different schools. I stayed at this school in Year 2 for two weeks and got to know some of the children well. The staff were all nice too, which makes a big difference.

I travelled some distance to my next school and, I don't know whether it was the area it was in or what, but this was quite an experience. I was in Year 4 and it seemed the majority of this class had no respect for their class teacher.

He was trying to run the lesson, but there were children walking around the classroom aimlessly, others fiddling with anything that was in reach or emptying their pencil cases for no reason, some rocking dangerously on their chairs and so many talking to each other instead of listening to the teacher.

A couple of them got up and walked out without asking so I followed them to make sure they were safe. They told me they were going to the toilet so I went back into the classroom, but after a good 5 minutes they hadn't returned. I ended up searching all over the school for these two boys who had taken themselves to the playground and were hiding anywhere they could. What was going on? This is a first!

I asked them what they thought they were doing and to go back to class. Even though I did this in a fair but firm manner one of their replies was "You can't tell us what to do, you're just a TA". I was shocked that such young children would talk to an adult like this.

They were running away from me and laughing for about 10 minutes (which felt more like an hour) when a member of staff came to help after seeing me from their window. He clearly had some sort of authority and they went straight back to class. Or perhaps it was that he was a recognised face to them and I wasn't?

Had I failed already? I felt like a failure anyway. I continued the day, but felt constantly stressed with the awful behaviour in that class for which there were no consequences, not sent to the Head's office or given a warning or anything.

I had hoped this was the one and only time I would witness this sort of behaviour and hear such rudeness, but little did I know, this was just the beginning!

CHAPTER 8

I was invited back to this same school, but in the nursery for a day so I thought I'd give it a go. Having been there now I realise why the school children were the way they were.

This nursery was really badly lead with no structure and barely a routine. The toys were so filthy I didn't want to touch them, but staff seemed happy enough to let the children put them in their mouths and dribble all over them, even worse was runny noses wiped on their hands while playing with equipment.

I was trying desperately to blow noses and wash hands if I saw a child in this position, but so many of them were like this that it was really difficult to keep on top of. They all seemed to have a cold of sorts.

Not only were the toys dirty, quite a few of them were damaged or even broken. When I pointed this out I was told to "Just put them away, they're fine". How can children be expected to play with toys in this condition?

When it came to 'tidy up time' the toys were quickly put away by staff without being washed or even wiped down. I was looked at in a very strange way when I asked where the cloths were and they replied by telling me that the toys and equipment only got washed every half term, as they didn't have time during a nursery day, and the cloths they had were only used to wipe the tables clean. I couldn't believe it, how disgusting!

I noticed there was very little interaction between staff and children during free play time with a few of the staff chatting to each other with their backs to the room so unable to see what was going on. Some children were using equipment in an unsafe manner, but this was unnoticed by anyone other than me.

When I said to the staff about it I got the reply "Well they've got to learn somehow". Yes I get that, but surely not by brandishing toys as weapons and using them to hit other children with? My reaction was dismissed by sighs and raised eyebrows as though they'd heard it all before and were passed caring.

I was relieved when it came to story time and most of the children did sit quietly for this at first, but the lady who was reading the story read it so quickly and with no changing tone to her voice that she may as well have been reading the Yellow Pages and they wouldn't have known.

Needless to say they became fidgety and bored with several leaving the group and nobody following them to ensure their safety so I too left the story time so that I could see these children and what they were doing. Nobody else seemed bothered.

It really wasn't that long ago that I was running my nurseries, but it was so very different. We all ensured that we spent quality time with the children in our care, teaching them everything they needed to know to set them up for school life. Respect towards each other, adults and our equipment was high up there, and at tidy up time all the children were involved so it wasn't just a staff job.

When 'free play' came into force it was even more necessary that they tidied away as soon as they had finished playing with whatever they had chosen otherwise there would have been toys all over the place, making the nursery not only unsafe, but also horribly untidy and we found that "a clean and tidy nursery was a happy nursery".

I've only been to a few different nurseries since starting with the agency, but there's definitely a running theme - young, inexperienced staff with no enthusiasm or commitment to their role. As for the 'Individual Child Profiles' that they have to fill in, I've come to realise that agency staff are asked to come in for a day just so that regular staff have time to complete them.

I appreciate that there are some settings where one member of staff may have between 9 and 12 children each to assess and this is time consuming, but to take your eye off the ball and leave agency to virtually run the place while they're ticking boxes is very concerning.

There certainly does seem to be a lot more paperwork in place now than in my day and I don't envy them for it, but the clue's in the name 'childcare' and that's not happening in some of my experiences so far.

For the next month or so I was backwards and forwards to nurseries I had been to before and wasn't really looking forward to returning to any of them, but as nothing else was available I didn't have a choice. What is it with these agencies keep sending me to nurseries, despite having told them several times that I would rather be in a school?

There must be other staff on their books that have equal experience or at least some experience with pre-school children. By this stage I'm starting to get fed up with it. Everywhere I go it's the same thing and I come home upset, frustrated, annoyed etc etc. This isn't what I signed up for. Thank goodness it's Christmas. Perhaps next year will be a new start?

CHAPTER 9

B ut no! My first job of the new year is another nursery, a new one for me, but still. I remember the weather being shockingly cold so scraping my car was a priority before going anywhere, which took a lot longer than anticipated as hard ice was stuck to it.

This setting wasn't too far away, but there was no choice than to drive through a very busy town so I got caught in commuter traffic and was late. I hate being late anywhere, when it comes to work, especially somewhere new.

As it was, I wasn't alone. I actually arrived before two of the regular staff so I was thanked as it was just me and the manager when the children started to arrive and she couldn't have let them in if it had been just her on her own. This is another setting that's difficult to find with parking a long way away. Not a good start all round for this one.

Most of the children here were lovely to work with and played nicely with all the toys and each other, a joy to be a part of after previous experiences. It was a clean and well presented setting.

My main memory of this place was that the outside area had to be used in all settings now, whatever the weather, and I was asked to supervise the children that chose to play outdoors.

It was absolutely freezing and, even with plenty of warm clothes, big coat, scarf, hat and gloves it was bitter and not at all enjoyable. I must have been out there for a good hour and a half when I was finally relieved, by which time I was not happy. Different children were coming and going, but nobody took over from me.

I could see the other staff through the window the whole time I was outside and they didn't appear to be doing much other than huddling around the radiators. I asked a couple of times if I could switch with one of them as it was so cold, but they said they were busy and needed to be inside to supervise their 'Profile' children. I couldn't see much of that going on, they just took full advantage of me being there.

It was a continual flow of different children choosing to play outside so I did get to spend time with most of them and they were delightful, I just didn' like the staff's attitude. I was only there for the morning and haven't returned. It took me the rest of the afternoon to defrost and stop shivering.

I had been sent an email offering me a role at a nursery within a school which was local. It was refeshing to know in advance what was on offer and not to get those early morning phone calls. I accepted and stayed at this setting for a month. It was split into two rooms, one for 2 to 3 year olds and one for 3 to 4 year olds, all on ground level with separate gardens for each group. It was nice.

The equipment and toys appeared clean and the children came in and got stuck into playing quickly and happily. Finally I was in a nursery that seemed organised and well managed with all the staff engaging with the children.

It was so good to see adults actually sitting at tables interacting with children and seemingly happy in their job. It reminded me of my nurseries and how we used to work and I could breathe a sigh of relief that this was going to be a place I would enjoy.

The most noticeable difference between this setting and others I had been to was the age of the staff. Here they were all mature ladies, similar to my age, some slightly younger, some a little older. Let's just say I would think we were nearly all menopausal here. Maybe that's what made it more enjoyable? Lots of things in common and knowing how to behave and talk appropriately around children.

There was no bitching, no standing around gossiping, no sitting around doing nothing. They were all quick to intervene if there looked like trouble brewing (which was rare) and all worked really well together, putting the children's safety and happiness first.

This made me even more convinced that it's an age thing. No amount of training and courses can compare with experience of your own children and general life skills which are acquired along the way of growing up. And, of course, good old fashioned common sense.

CHAPTER 10

Iwent to a couple of new settings for me which were some distance away and didn't enjoy any of them. It's beginning to sound like I'm in the wrong job I know, but it's not just me that can see the obvious.

I've worked with many agency staff or even regular staff in lots of cases, that have not been happy in the workplace. A certain look can tell what people are thinking, words don't have to be used, and these looks were getting more and more frequent at different nurseries and schools.

I had been at a couple of settings where an Ofsted Inspection was taking place and the difference in the behaviour of everyone was unbelievable. Suddenly staff who barely spoke and were always glum had lots to say, were overly smiley and were keen to interact with the children. The settings were clean and tidy with lots of children's art work on the walls and hanging up, whereas very little had been on the walls before.

It's all for show and as soon as the Inspections are over, it's back to normal. There should be cameras in these places for higher authorities to see what goes on when they're not there, not just what they see when they visit as that's not always real.

I've often thought it would be good to be a Spy for the authorities. An agency worker would have the ideal opportunity if that job was ever needed, I would be first in line.

I was feeling like my recent training and refresher courses were going to waste as I hadn't had any offers for 1-2-1 work when at last I got an email offering me such a position for one week at a fairly local school with a Year 3 boy. Was this going to be the start of something new for me? I really hoped so as I was done with nursery.

Excitement and nerves had taken over my body and my heart was pounding when I arrived. Although I had been to quite a few schools by now and seen Supply staff working with SEN children, this was my very first time which was a huge responsibility.

I was introduced to the class and the boy I was supporting, who was quiet, but happy to have me at his side to help him with the curriculum. We bonded quite quickly and found things out about each other so that I was a person to him and not 'just a TA'!

He appeared to like my way of working with him and it was so rewarding when he understood something, a few real lightbulb moments which, hopefully will stay with him forever. This happened a few times throughout the week and I felt satisfied that I had achieved this with him.

He particularly liked it when we worked outside. I will take any opportunity to be outdoors and he too enjoyed that. I remember getting a few funny looks from staff, but we were both happy and he was learning and responding which was the main thing. He also seemed much more able and willing to do his learning outside rather than inside, whatever the subject. That's my kind of work.

Since then there is 'outdoor learning' and 'forest schools' in most, if not all schools now so maybe I started a trend without even realising it? We all know that fresh air is good for us and to be surrounded by nature while learning, so it always made sense to me to be outdoors as often as possible. I love reading stories to children in the sunshine or doing any kind of work that is possible away from the classroom.

It wasn't all easy though as it was overshadowed by the behaviour of one boy in particular in that class, who just had to be the centre of attention the whole time. If he wasn't interrupting the teacher he was rocking on his chair in a very unsafe manner, disturbing other children or generally causing chaos within this class.

He was the one who needed support I felt. It was so unfair on all the other children who wanted to listen and learn. Most tried to ignore him, but it wasn't easy. It must be so difficult for a teacher when this sort of behaviour is going on and the child will not listen to you.

I realised at playtime in the playground that there were many children here that had severe behaviour issues and I actually felt quite threatened at times from some of them. Surely I shouldn't feel like this with young children should I?

The first time I was on the playground I had to separate two boys who, I'm sure, would have started fighting if I hadn't intervened. I put myself between the two of them so that they couldn't reach each other, even though they were waving their fists and gritting their teeth, by which time there was quite a crowd.

A male member of staff came to my rescue, but this was a horrible experience for my first day here. I was on playground duty for the rest of the week and dreaded it every day as there was always something going on which wasn't good. I was glad to be back in the class or our chosen outdoor space with my nice quiet boy who wanted to learn.

CHAPTER 11

I visited a couple more new nurseries over the next month or so with that same old feeling, then gave myself a break over the half term, even though I had been offered several full day care setting roles. I took this time to re-evalute my future as I knew I wasn't happy, infact I was really getting very low to the point I thought I needed to see a doctor.

I struggled to explain how I was feeling to her as I just couldn't stop crying. I had often driven home from work in tears (which isn't safe) and I no longer felt like me. Was it the job, was it the menopause or a combination of both? She diagnosed me with depression, which really just made me feel even sadder. I was put on antidepressants which made my weight balloon, making me feel even worse.

I have really dark thoughts, most of which I couldn't possibly share with anyone. I often wonder if there's something more wrong with me than the diagnosed depression. Actually, the more people I meet along the way the more I think everyone is 'on the spectrum' or has some kind of condition. We're all different and should respect that.

I don't know if it's getting older that I've noticed it more or if it is the case, but so many people are difficult to communicate with or you feel like you're treading on eggshells when you talk to them.

Nobody can do or say anything anymore without somebody being offended. It's a difficult world we live in. And as for text messaging. It's so easy for people to misinterpret what's written depending on their mood!

When I was young my mum would often say that she felt stressed, anxious and depressed, but they were just words at the time as I was too young to really understand. She would burst into tears for what seemed like no reason, or I could see that she had been crying and was trying to get on with things. She started her menopause at 41, which is very young, and now I can completely relate to how she had been feeling for so many years. I just wish I had known at the time.

For my own sanity I felt I needed to steer clear of any previous nurseries I had been to and start a fresh elsewhere. I started back after the half term with a long week, 8am to 6pm at two different day care nurseries. I really tried hard to go in with a positive attitude, but this quickly went when I entered busy rooms with lots of screaming toddlers.

It's hard to enjoy a job when there's so much chaos going on around you. To keep me going I kept thinking that I would get a school job soon, but time passed and it was one nursery after another. I was even kind of wishing I was back in that playground with the children who were nearly fighting! At least there I was in a school and not a nursery.

I worked through the summer holidays at different settings, most of which were full day care as that's all that's available during holidays. I put my head down and got on with it, trying to spend as much time as possible with children instead of cleaning and tidying all the time, but I do enjoy keeping a place nice and neat so this was ongoing everywhere I went as nobody else seemed to bother too much!

I would busy myself as much as possible to make the days go quicker and enjoyed the company of a lot of the children. There are a lot of sweet children out there, despite everything.

I don't know if it's because I am quite often a new face, but I find many children head in my direction wherever I am in a room and want to play with or near me.

I'm certainly not blowing my own trumpet, but it does make you feel good when people want to be with you. I have a calm manner and always get down to a child's level which is less intimidating for them rather than looking up at adults, and I am tall, so further up than most.

I also like to make them feel good about themselves with whatever they produce, whether it's something they've built out of bricks or created out of playdoh or anything inbetween. There's nothing like a bit of praise and a big smile to boost someone's confidence, especially a child's.

Although the way I'm feeling at this moment in time I find smiling somewhat of an effort! I can now understand a bit of why those ladies on my very first day were looking so sullen.

This kind of work really takes it out of you emotionally, but it's not so much the children as the staff and the rules and the lack of discipline which gives children the freedom to think they can do what they like.

A lot of the children may have things going on at home that we don't know about which make them the way they are. No one knows what goes on behind closed doors, unfortunately. They may be subjected to a form of abuse or hold some kind of trauma. It's horrible to think about, but I do think there must be things going on in their lives to make them behave the way they do.

I thought about doing criminology or child psychology when I was younger, but am kind of glad I didn't as it must fill your head with so much upset. I am drawn to programmes that contain psychology and more often than not a troubled adult's life goes back to when they were a child as to how they've been moulded and why they are like they are. This is why I worry so much about some of the children I've worked with to date, let alone what's to come.

This was clearly a
seemed at all su
library or eve
in class. It
him. Fc
contr

CHA

For the next month I
I hadn't been to bef
and the other for 2 days as a general ... ...
quite nicely as I got to know both schools, their routine
and the children.

That's what's good about working for agencies. You can
pick and choose, if there is a choice, and have time off at
your own convenience, something that is not always
possible if you're a permanent member of staff. I chose to
work 5 days a week, but I have met many agency staff
who only wanted to work a couple of days a week or just
mornings or afternoons and this was the only way they
could do that.

Both of these schools were nice enough and the majority
of the children were well behaved and well mannered.
My 1-2-1 was a Year 1 boy who didn't seem to want to
be at school at all. No matter how much help I offered he
would spend most of his time doing anything to avoid
doing any actual work.

His work books were as good as empty, while others in
the class were almost full, and he would frequently leave
the room without asking so I would have to follow him
everywhere to make sure he was safe.

gular occurance as none of the staff
rised to see him in the corridors or the
he playground when he should have been
emed to be purely a behaviour thing with
one so young he wanted to be in complete
of everything he did.

although I was asked to stay on after my first month I
declined as I just felt I wasn't getting anywhere with him.
He didn't want to learn and all I was doing was walking
around after him like a lapdog. I hadn't done years of
training for this. I was no more than babysitting.

Inbetween all this negativity there are lots of good things
that happen in schools too, otherwise I think I would
have left by now. It's the funny things children say that
make the day worthwhile. During one of the brief
opportunities I was actually in the classroom at this
school we were talking about what they would like to do
as a job when they grow up.

There were a few that said "I want to work like my
Dad", but when asked, they had no idea what he did," he
just works". Others wanted to be a teacher (God help
them) or Doctor or a singer, but the one I remember the
most was a boy who said he wanted to be a "Binman".
The teacher asked why and he replied "Because they only
work on Fridays so I can play on my XBox the rest of
the time".

CHAPTER 13

I was sort of excited and apprehensive about the next role that was offered as it was at a private SEN school with only 7 - 9 children in each class because of the severity of their needs. Although I had come across a lot of SEN children over the years, either in nurseries or schools, this was my first experience of a school specifically for these children.

At first I thought I was out of my depth with this one, but I quickly got into it and just followed the directions I was given by the experienced staff. I was asked to support one child who was 13 years old, which was much older than any other child I had worked with.

He was nearly as tall as me and quite a big lad in build. He was extremely unpredictable so one minute he would be sitting down listening to the class teacher and the next he would start shouting or pick things up and throw them. His needs weren't the most severe in this class either and I had begun wishing I had worn a hard hat as things were randomly thrown across the room often.

I got the impression that none of these youngsters liked new people, they liked their routine and knowing who was who. I did feel intimated by some of them, especially the ones that squared up to me and had their face very close to mine.

It's hard to know how to react to something like that when it's the first time it's ever happened, but I was told by the staff that they were just checking me out and I should remain calm and friendly, which is what I did, even though inside I was shaking as I didn't know what they would do next.

I did return to this school a few times after and I felt I learnt a lot from the way staff treated these children and their patience and understanding towards all their individual needs. They all had a unique way of teaching and were a credit to that school.

Each time I went there I was with different children in different classes so I think I went to all of them eventually. It certainly wouldn't be a place I would want to be on a permanent basis, but to go back every now and then was nice and I felt more confident each time.

I was offered a role at a Children's Centre during the half term and was told that there were mainly SEN children at this centre. Having now been at the previous private school I felt fairly confident that this would be similar in its style of teaching, but how wrong was I?

For a start there was no teaching. These were all children on their half term break, but needed somewhere to go due to parents working or that they had funding for such a place, so it was more of a holiday camp, well for them anyway, it certainly wasn't like a holiday for me! I arrived before any of the children so that I could be briefed on how the day is run, if you can call it that!

All of the children who were expected in had their names on the blackboard and were crossed off as they arrived. I noticed a name that I recognised, but hoped to God it wasn't the same child. His name was still on the board 20 minutes after everyone else had come in so I thought perhaps he wasn't coming, but then I heard screaming and shouting in the hall and just knew that it was him.

This was a child I had come across at a school and was supported by different TA's each time I went there as he was very difficult to manage and too much for any one person for any length of time. I had always been relieved that I had never been asked to support him in school and now made myself occupied so that I wouldn't be asked this time. I was already with two children and I could see the manager looking around for someone to help with him.

He is mildly autistic, but mainly it's his severe behaviour that sets him apart. He wouldn't think anything of picking up a chair and throwing it across a room if he got angry and didn't care who was in the way. In school I saw him violently swipe an entire shelf of all it's equipment and then jump on that shelf.

He's not a small boy and his actions were always very aggressive. It was always left to an adult to clear up his mess though, I never once saw him be told to clear up himself.

He would be taken to the Head's office several times a day where he was given therapy toys to play with. I don't see this as punishment. He was in a mainstream school and the other children were witness to his constant bad behaviour and could see the outcome which was him being rewarded with toys!

As the day went on at the Children's Centre I became increasingly wary and concerned at things that were going on. Adults/staff were throwing things across the room to children and running around the room playing chase. This seemed to make all the children go wild and soon everyone was running around and jumping off of things. This was a Centre for all ages so some of these youngsters were at secondary school and were like mini adults, some not even so mini!

I could almost feel my jaw on the floor and felt really unsafe as most of these children had no spatial awareness and were kicking equipment out of the way as they were running. All the regular staff were involved in this, but me and another agency lady just couldn't believe what was happening.

I was scared for my own safety as well as the safety of all the children as some of them were running way too fast for indoors. I felt like I was in a lunatic asylum and I just wanted to get out, but it was only 10.30am and I was there until 4pm!! HELP

When things did calm down I asked the manager if this was some kind of activity, even though it appeared random. She informed me that these children need to be physical so it's best for them if they can let off steam by having a good run around. I can completely understand that, but surely it would be much better in an empty hall or even outside, not in a hall that's full of equipment which was being kicked and thrown around?

It happened again shortly after lunch and this time it seemed even crazier. Maybe what they ate had an affect? If I hadn't seen it with my own eyes, I would have struggled to believe it, it really was wild and I've never been more pleased to see 4pm on the clock.

CHAPTER 14

I was offered another Children's Centre in a different area that same week and now knew that these were places of play. I accepted and met a really lovely TA who was with the same agency as me. We instantly hit it off and have since seen each other at many different schools.

It was good to be able to share how I felt about some of these nurseries, schools and Children's Centres, but even better to know that she felt the same, so it wasn't just me. We tried our best to control the bad behaviour that was shown at this centre between a lot of the children, but it seemed to be a lost cause.

There didn't appear to be any SEN children there, although there were a few of concern, but there was so much bad behaviour that was hardly taken any notice of. There seems to be a lot of "Make the right choices" coming from staff, but this made no difference. How can children learn if there are no consequences? I rarely see any children having any sort of punishment for their actions.

I'm not talking about the cane, like when I was a child, those were very different days - but we certainly learnt from it. It was more the humiliation than the pain as everybody seemed to know very quickly who was getting it and you could then see that their hand was red and sore or they couldn't sit down, depending on which part of the body the cane was given.

Thank goodness we've moved on from that, but have now gone to the extreme of no punishment or consequences, even rewarding bad behaviour, certainly from the schools and nurseries I've been to so far anyway.

I'm convinced that children should be taught right from wrong from the very beginning so when people say "They're too young to understand" I don't agree. My own boys learnt very quickly if they did or said anything inappropriate and grew to be polite and careful with everything, both their language and use of equipment.

Along with my staff at my nurseries we all taught every child that came through the door what was acceptable and what wasn't and they learnt quickly too. I feel that so many children nowadays haven't been taught the basic life skills, but it does all come from learned behaviour and so many parents are very young themselves - kids having kids!

CHAPTER 15

Back to another full day care nursery, this one was another first for me. I was very taken with the building itself as it was a huge old house, possibly a stately home and had wonderful huge grounds. The entrance hall alone was stunning with lots of original features so I was excited about exploring this place.

It was split into many different rooms depending on the ages of the children and there was a separate building for the babies. I was pleased that I was in a room with the pre-school children and not the babies as a first visit.

I was pointed in the direction of the room I would be in, but not taken there by anyone. I didn't mind as I'm now getting used to the ways these places operate. I did have to introduce myself as I entered the room though as nobody took any notice of me which made me slightly uncomfortable. I guess they saw my brightly coloured lanyard and knew I was there to help.

Being a new place for me I had no idea of their routine or what was expected of me so I straight away asked several questions of the room leader who was rushing around, but not for any particular reason really, just to look busy maybe?

I joined a group of children who were playing nicely in a creative area and they seemed happy that I was there. I did notice that none of the other adults in the room were with any of the children, they were all either doing their Child Profiles or just talking to each other. That said, all of the children did seem quite happy playing in their own little groups or on their own so perhaps adult intervention wasn't required all the time they were content.

It wasn't long before I was asked to start clearing the toys away to get ready for snack, but it was difficult to get the attention of any staff to help me find where things went so I had to look around for myself.

There must have been 4 permanent staff and 3 agency, including myself, due to the number of children in this room. The agency ladies were in a similar situation to me, having not been there before, so it was new to all of us, but none of us were told anything about the running of the room or their daily routine.

I've come to accept that these full day care nurseries spend a lot of the day eating, sleeping and toiletting, with play inbetween. This was a long day 8.30am to 6pm, but I felt I didn't spend much time interacting with any children as it was full on and constant either taking them to the toilet, changing nappies, helping them to sleep or helping them with their food courses.

Fortunately it was a lovely sunny day, if a bit chilly, so we did manage to get outside. Considering how long the day was though we were only outside for a little bit before lunch and again before home time. It seemed like such a waste of all the outside space they had, but they had their routine and it didn't include being outdoors much.

I went back to this setting quite a few times during this holiday and slowly got to know some of the staff, even though they seemed reluctant to engage. I don't know if it's because I'm older than most of them or if it's because I ask lots of questions, but my conversations were mainly with agency staff and not the permanents.

The staffroom at this place was in a small shed with long bench seats running either side of a table in the middle. I felt instantly uncomfortable with this arrangement, especially as nobody really spoke. I hate being in the middle of a row at the best of times. I like to be able to see a whole room without turning my head so I can observe everything and everybody.

A few of them were clearly friends outside of nursery and didn't seem shy in any way about talking of their nights out and what they did! I'm quite an open person and am rarely shocked, but some of the things I heard made my hair curl and I could feel myself cringing. How could young girls talk in this way?

The 'c' word was used like it was going out of fashion and every other word was the 'f' word. They could obviously control their use of language as they didn't talk like this around the children, so this came as a big shock to me.

My main memory of this nursery was when we were outside one day waiting for parents to collect the children. There is a lovely activity area where they play, with balancing beams, tunnels, climbing frames, slides etc, and this is where they are collected at the end of each day.

As usual most of the staff were talking to each other and not overly watching the children and I noticed a little girl underneath a climbing frame. She was in a safe space and seemed like she was just having a quiet moment to herself so I kept an eye on her while also watching out for others.

After she'd been there for about 10 minutes I thought I saw her eating something, but there was no food out so this seemed strange. Maybe she had sneaked something in her pocket? I had seen her a few times before, but not worked in the room she's in, and she did come across as neglected from what I saw. Her hair was always very messy and knotty and her clothes were old and tatty.

I bent down to her level to see what she was doing and saw that she was holding what looked like some sort of chocolate bar, but on closer inspection was horrified to find that she had done a poo and was eating it!!!

The only other time I've seen anything like this was at a wildlife park when a chimpanzee did a poo and then ate it like it was a bar of chocolate. It seemed a very natural thing for the chimp to do, but everyone watching was repulsed. This was an almost identical act, but this was a child that was doing it, not a chimpanzee!

I stood up and waved the manager over without drawing attention to what was happening as I didn't want everyone, especially the other children, knowing what she was doing. When the manager came over I told her about it and she wasn't surprised. Apparently this wasn't the first time this little girl had done this.

She was taken inside by a member of staff who works in her room to be cleaned up. Apart from a couple of the staff members saying that it was disgusting it wasn't spoken about or reported as far as I was aware.

I did my job in reporting it to the manager to deal with, but wasn't asked to fill in any paperwork or report it to the owner or anything. This was 5 years ago. There would definitely be a child protection report drawn up now if that happened, and should have been then too by rights, especially something like that.

I never did find out the history of this building as nobody knew anything about it or seemed to care, not even the owners.

CHAPTER 16

I gave myself the last 10 days of the summer holidays off for a much needed break away before starting the Autumn Term, not knowing where I would be going.

I was asked to attend a school quite far away for just 1 day with an SEN child, but hadn't been informed of the severity of his condition. It was only when I arrived and was introduced to the boy that I knew this was beyond my training and any experience.

Although this was a mainstream school this boy was wheelchair bound, couldn't communicate in any way and needed regular toiletting with at least 2 people to help. Surely he should have been in a Special Needs School? I got through the day with a lot of support, but this was an extremely challenging day both physically and mentally.

Over the next month or so I went to several different schools, some for just a day and others for a few days. Most were working with Key Stage 1 children as a general TA and some with SEN children whose needs were fairly mild.

I certainly came across a lot of unusual names during my time at schools to say the least and have noticed that even the simplest of names like Amy have several different ways of spelling i.e. A-i-m-e-e, A-m-i-e, A-i-m-y, A-m-i. Do parents not think before they name their child that they will have to go through life spelling it on every occasion?

Whenever I write a child's name on their artwork, if they can't do it themselves, I always have to ask a member of staff how it's spelt so that I don't just assume and 9 times out of 10 it's spelt differently to how you would expect.

I've met a brother and sister whose names have been royal titles, a boy who was named after a football stadium and a girl with the longest non-English name I've ever come across with almost as many letters in as our alphabet.

I've met every season, every flower, bodies of water and every celebration. They may be interesting and often unique names, but come on, as if children haven't got enough to worry about with schooling they've got these names to live with and spell out!

I've also noticed that there's definitely something in a name and every school I go to staff say the same thing. People can't know when they give a baby a name how they're going to turn out, but I just know that if a child has a certain name that they're going to be 'difficult' and this applies mainly to boys. It's very odd, but very true.

A lot of children's accents also seem to be changing. I've worked with many that I thought were American, but it turns out that they watch so much American TV, Youtube clips or Games on the Xbox etc that they've picked up this way of talking. Unbelievable really.

CHAPTER 17

I was at my next new school for a full week and, to date, this was one of the loveliest schools I've been to and I really enjoyed my time there. It was the smallest I've ever visited with only 4 teachers and 2 TA's. The staffroom was friendly and welcoming and I instantly felt part of their small team.

It was a religious school and every morning started with an assembly and prayers. All the children were impressively well behaved and there was no fidgetting or fiddling about either in the assembly or in their classrooms. They all responded well to their teachers and seemed very happy to be there.

I don't know if I just got lucky the time I was there in that they didn't have any children with needs, including bad behaviour, or if it was the way the school was managed, but it was a breath of fresh air and an absolute joy to work there.

If it hadn't been such a pain to get to I would definitely have asked the agency if I could have stayed on or returned when needed, but the journey to this school was a very stressful start to the day.

I tried several different ways to get there, but some were worse than others. Due to commuter traffic and having to drive through a major town it took at least an hour and that was on a good day, but only 20 minutes to get home.

School holidays again so back to a few nursery schools. I have been to so many now that I know what to expect and also informed the agency of the ones I simply didn't want to return to. It's great being agency as you can be honest and let them know your reasons for either wanting to stay or not wanting to go back. They always ask for feedback and sometimes I can be a bit too honest, but I think if you don't tell them they won't know.

CHAPTER 18

I was beginning to get fed up going to different places all the time and felt it would be a good experience to stay in one school for a period of time, whether it was a term or the full school year, so when the agency offered me this option I jumped at it.

I went along for a visit to meet the staff and the child I would be supporting who was in Year 3. As this would be a long term role it was important for all of us that I was right for this job. The visit went well and I was really excited.

This particular school had a good reputation. Even when I had my nurseries it was a school that parents wanted their children to go to. I knew nothing about it really as it's not in my area, but driving past it every day on route home from one of my nurseries I could see the children coming in and out and thinking how sweet they looked, the boys in their little blazers and the girls with their bonnets and pinafore dresses, adorable.

As part of this school routine all the children with SEN (and there were a lot of them) went into a room on arrival to start their day with a small assault course. They would do a physical activity then move on to the next. I just observed the girl I was working with before properly being introduced.

This wasn't a particularly big room, but there was a lot going on and I could feel myself getting hot and bothered by it all. Nobody spoke to me and I felt like a spare part. I tried talking to some of the staff, but it was like pulling teeth. I'm not sure about this one.

I'm going to refer to this child as 'M' rather than the little girl. After the assault course I walked with M towards her classroom. We asked each other a few questions on the way to find things out about each other and she ended up giving me a guided tour of the school, including the playground. I had checked that this was ok to do so and was told by the Senior SEN Leader that she would be happier doing this than being in class.

M took me round the whole school and pointed out all the different rooms and showed delight in being able to do this as she was in control. The first few days with her weren't too bad. She did a little bit of work in her books in the classroom, which she didn't do very often apparently.

I had been warned that she was very unpredictable, but not noticed anything initially. Infact she came across as quite a sweet little thing who just wanted some attention.

We ended up in a small room which she said was 'her room'. It was very bare with just a tall, plastic lava style lamp with fish and bubbles in, a few books and lots of soft toys. There was nothing on the walls apart from a few lumps taken out of them.

We sat on the floor and I read her a story which she clearly enjoyed, snuggling up to me and sucking her thumb. When I finished it she wanted me to read it again, but I suggested we go to her class as I hadn't met her teacher yet and she was missing her learning. This didn't go down too well and she suddenly changed personality.

She got angry and said she didn't want to go to class, but somehow we got there and she sat in her seat at the back of the room. I sat next to her and the teacher acknowledged us with a nod and carried on with the lesson, which was coming to an end as we had been so long touring the school.

I was on playground duty at breaktime and got talking to a staff member. When I told her who I was supporting she wished me luck and said that many had tried and failed. I didn't like the sound of this, but at the same time I felt a challenge coming on.

My first week was a success. I had got her into the classroom straight after the assault course and even got her to do some writing and drawing in her work books, which had very little in them. I tried to make everything exciting or to sound like she was missing out which seemed to work.

I was praised by the class teacher for how much I had got out of her in such a short time. It soon became clear that this was just a settling in period for both of us, getting to know each other and how things work, as it was downhill from here.

I dreaded going into the SEN room every morning as it was not a nice atmosphere. The 1-2-1 staff were as miserable as sin and the room leader was very hard work in that she rarely spoke to anyone and when she did it seemed like an effort. She was only young, but I never saw her smile once and clearly didn't like her job.

This school was like St Trinians. When the children came in in the morning with their little blazers and bonnets they would take them off and throw them on the floor below their pegs in the corridors. Hardly anything was hung on pegs. I've seen Jumble Sales tidier than this school's corridor.

I witnessed children jumping on tables and chairs when the teacher wasn't in the room and this was happening all over the school in all year groups. This behaviour combined with the volume of them shouting was horrible.

It was mad. Children running through the corridors shouting and screaming, often very rude words. None of the staff seemed to have any sort of control and it was a domino effect in that one started they all followed. I thought the Children's Centre was bad enough, but at least that had an excuse that they were all SEN and it was a place to play. This was a mainstream school, it was crazy.

There was one member of staff who was new, started at the same time as me, only she was permanent and not agency. We got talking and quickly became friends. She had never worked in a school before so had nothing to compare it to, but I assured her that they were not all like this, infact this was a really bad example of how a school should be with the lack of control and punishment. These children were ruling the roost and they knew it.

All the 1-2-1 staff were following their children around like lapdogs while the children were running out of class, in the corridors and the playground. Unless you had 'Positive Touch' training you weren't allowed to touch the child and that included putting a hand to them to guide them into class. It was a joke. Way too much red tape.

M had started to show her true colours and I could see why 'her room' was so bare. When she got angry she would pick something up and throw it across the room. This was usually a book rather than a cuddly toy as she knew it would cause more damage.

There had been more things in this room once upon a time, but she damaged everything so they had to be removed. I realised the lumps in the walls were where books and other objects had hit it and she had even thumped and kicked it too.

When M was off school, which was quite often, I supported a year 5 boy who was a shocker for bad behaviour. He was very much a part of a double act with another year 5 boy. They were in the same class at first, but were split up after they couldn't sit, or be in the same room together without causing havoc.

The classrooms were both next to each other and when one of the boys left the room he would leap about at the window of the other classroom door to get the attention of his friend who would then leave his class and the two of them would run all over the school thinking it was hilarious that teachers and TA's were chasing them.

I refused to chase after him as this is exactly what he wanted. I just made sure I could always see him and would try to entice him back to class which rarely worked. He was a child who did his own thing and would not take notice of anyone trying to help.

Quite why he was in school I don't know as he was always out of the class fooling around with his friend. None of the staff had any control over either of them.

When they were together they both ignored the adults, even when we were right in their face talking to them. It was like we were invisible. They were rude, had no respect and no manners. Swearing came naturally and they were impossible to reprimand. Everything was on their terms only.

I had a few nice moments with M, but most of my memories were not good. She wasn't allowed in Assembly as she was so unpredictable, along with quite a few other children. Luckily she usually didn't go anywhere near the hall when this was taking place so I didn't have to worry, but one day she just flew down the corridor and into the hall where she ran in and out of the children, who were all sitting on the floor, stepping on and over them and laughing.

She was small in stature and very quick when she wanted to be. I was absolutely mortified by her actions, but then it got worse. She ran to the front of the room and grabbed the candle snuffler then ran among the children again, this time bashing them on the head with the snuffler as she went, laughing all the time.

Many of the children were getting upset by this and it seemed to go on forever. It took 3 of us to catch her, although a lot more staff were trying. And of course it had to be staff who were 'Positive Touch' trained and not just any of us, despite the dangerous position she was putting the other children in!

She was taken to the Head's office for a talk about her behaviour and then given some therapy toys to play with to calm her down. I stayed with her the whole time and felt she was being rewarded by what she had just done as there was no punishment, no consequences, nothing, just toys to play with and a brief talking to. It must be the new thing.

I was only about 5 weeks in and had worked with the year 5 boy often. His class teacher was a lovely young lady who had not long completed her training, having spent thousands of pounds and hundreds of hours in doing so, but I could see she was not happy about the behaviour of lots of the children in her class, especially him.

She seemed close to tears on several occasions and then one day she just burst when we alone. She sobbed like a baby and I hugged her for what seemed like the longest time. Teaching wasn't what she thought it would be and she was regretting her years of training if this is what it was going to be like.

I assured her that this school was a really bad example and that there are a lot of schools out there are well managed and enjoyable to work in. She handed in her notice at the end of the term and I hope, wherever she went, that she's still teaching and is happy now. It would be a real shame if that school and those few children put her off teaching completely.

M was getting more and more difficult to work with and every day something would happen. I was reading her a story in 'her room' which she always seemed to really enjoy. I got the impression that this doesn't happen at home.

She was snuggled up to me, sucking her thumb and appeared engrossed in the story when she suddenly decided to grab my arm and give me a Chinese burn. This really hurt and I was shocked at how out of the blue this came.

She then started screaming and kicking the walls. For her own safety, and the safety of others, I felt I should keep her in the room by standing at the door. The handle was up high for security, but she was trying to climb up me to reach it.

I had no phone or radio to call for help and it was only when a member of staff walked by that I knocked for her attention. She then came back with 2 other staff members to help me with M. I felt extremely vulnerable in this situation and really quite scared. Should I be scared of a tiny girl?

Working at this school certainly didn't help with my depression, in fact I was as low as I've ever been and would cry my eyes out as soon as I got home or usually as soon as I got out of the school gates most days.

I tried really hard not to let these children get to me, but it didn't get any better. How could children make me, and so many other adults, so miserable? I went into childcare because of my love for them, their innocence, their wanting to learn and the amusing things they come out with. This was very different and I had little love left.

By this stage I had made my mind up that I was going to leave this school at the end of the term. I was supposed to have been there for the academic year, but it was making me ill and so unhappy that it just wasn't worth it. Another advantage to being agency, you can leave when you like without notice.

I went in every day with a good mindset, but it would never be long before I was drained. I tried so hard to get something out of M, but everything was on her terms. It was her way or no way.

I used to just follow her around going where she wanted to go and doing what she wanted to do. I felt that I was wasted as a TA/SENCO in this role as I wasn't able to get her in the class to do any work.

There's a song with the lyrics 'If it don't feel good what are you doing it for?' and I thought that would be a good motto to live by. It certainly doesn't feel good at the moment and God only knows why I'm doing it.

We would talk often and find out about each other. We discussed our favourite things like animals, colours, music etc and she would remember things I told her, as I did about her too.

There were times when she could be so lovely, but her unpredictability was like nothing I've ever come across before, or since. She reminded me of 'The Little Girl with the Little Curl' 'When she was good she was very very good and when she was bad she was horrid'.

We were having a chat one day in 'her room' and she seemed really quite content when suddenly she grabbed my glasses off of my head pulling a chunk of hair out at the same time. The pain was intense and I was very close to tears, but I didn't want to give her the satisfaction of knowing she had hurt me so I somehow managed to stifle it.

She broke my expensive glasses and thought the whole thing was funny. I've learnt my lesson from this. I now only wear cheap glasses to schools and keep my good ones for home. I was never compensated for them or even given any sort of sympathy from the Head for how she made me feel.

The final straw came when we were walking down a corridor towards her classroom. She was holding my hand and skipping, showing that she appeared to be happy, when all of a sudden she backed up and then karate kicked me in my lower stomach. She completely winded me and this action was witnessed by a member of staff who looked horrified.

This time I couldn't hide the pain and the tears. I have had two caesarians and been opened up on the same scar another two times for other reasons so am very tender and sensitive in that area. She wasn't to know that of course, but even so, that's not something a child should do to an adult, especially for no reason.

This incident happened right outside the staffroom so I was able to go in there quickly to vent my pain while M was being dealt with by the SEN leader. I could hear her screaming and refusing to go with the adult, but I was passed caring and just wanted to go home.

I never returned to this school after this, but often wonder how those children are now. I would like to think that they are growing up into nice young people, but somehow I doubt it. I think I'm more likely to see most of them on Crimewatch or Britain's Most Wanted!!

The lady I had become friends with was getting increasingly fed up too so I suggested doing agency work instead so that she would get an insight into how other schools are managed. She gave notice and joined the agency I'm with and has never looked back.

She worked in several different schools before settling at one for a long term role and she is very happy. This school was an experience for us to say the least, one that I wouldn't want to repeat and one that still gives me shudders when I think about it or drive near it.

In all these schools with weak leadership I feel for the children as it does only seem to be the minority who are difficult, but it's them that take over. So many children want to learn and want to be in school, but it's so hard for them when the much attention is on those who don't.

CHAPTER 19

Whilst it was a huge relief to have left that last school, the damage had already been done. I was at a point where I didn't want to see anybody socially, not even my very best friends. I wouldn't answer my phone as I didn't want to speak to anyone. If I did find myself in a social circle I had nothing to say and felt permanently close to tears.

In fact I would often have to leave the social situation to return home to cry myself to sleep or, if we had friends over, I would just disappear upstairs without saying goodnight so that I didn't have to try. It was awful and so out of character for me. It's hard work trying to look cheerful and be chatty when inside your head is scrambled and sad.

Me and my family are very close and very social, often having parties, big or small, and nearly always having different friends over at the weekends for drinks in the garden in the Summer or gathering in the kitchen when the weather wasn't good, so this new side of me was very different and I didn't like it. I was changing beyond recognition.

I thought I did a good job at hiding it for as long as I could, but I'm not that good an actress and I had to eventually tell my nearest and dearest that I was suffering with depression and anxiety. It was a shock to a lot of them, but everyone was so supportive.

You find out who your real friends are at times like this and I found myself surrounded by love and kindness which helped enormously. I will be forever grateful to my husband, my boys, my sister and all my friends for sticking with me and getting me through that horrendous time.

The menopause feels like it's going on forever as well, which really doesn't help. People always talk about the hot flushes, but there's so much more to it. I thought I was getting early Dementia, but no, forgetfulness is one of the symptoms, along with not being able to make simple choices, crying at the drop of a hat, everything and everyone getting on your nerves (no matter how much you love them) and general brain fog.

On top of all that you've got a change in your body shape, everything drying up (and I mean everything!!), unable to sleep, reduced or non-existent sex drive and always grumpy. And why does even the word 'menopause' have to have 'men' in it? Can't we have something that's not about them?

All that said, the depression still comes back every now and then, but nothing like it was. I now have moments of depression as opposed to permanently. It makes a huge difference to what's going on in my life and how happy I am at work so I am now very choosy about which schools I work in as I don't want to feel as low as I was during this period ever again.

I chose not to work in any nursery schools in the Summer holidays and gave myself a complete break. Me and my husband enjoyed a wonderful 10 day holiday in Italy and I spent every day when we were at home in my garden which is my happy place.

I love getting new plants and repotting existing ones, listening and watching the birds and squirrels and generally appreciating what I've got. There's nothing quite like a morning coffee in the garden listening to the dawn chorus, apart from perhaps a glass of wine in the evening listening to the birdsong.

When I was deeply unhappy I just wanted to get away from where I lived thinking that would make things better. I was sick and tired of looking at the same things day in day out, going on the same walks and seeing the same people.

I've lived in the same village all my life. Being depressed and menopausal is not a good combination! But I am so lucky with where I live and what I've got and every now and then I give myself a good talking to about this.

CHAPTER 20

I was somewhat reluctant to return to work for the Autumn Term having had such a lovely Summer break, but I had been offered an ongoing role at a school I had been to a couple of times before which I had thoroughly enjoyed so I went for it.

Everyone there made me feel welcomed back and said how good it was to see me again. This was doing wonders for my confidence. I was advised by the class teachers what was expected of me and most of the time I would be working in my own little area with a variety of children, from Reception, Year 1 and Year 2, sometimes just with one child and sometimes in groups. This was a really nice, varied way of working and all the children were delightful.

The staff couldn't have been friendlier and I was really happy there. The only downside was that to get to this school I had to drive by the last one so would often see some of the children walking in or out in their blazers and bonnets. I was so glad I wasn't there anymore, but it did make me very anxious every time I saw them and would wonder who was supporting them and how they were getting on. I don't think I'll ever forget that school!

Not only was this new school I was at friendly and supportive, I was also given a whole hour for my lunchbreak. This was a first in any schools or nurseries I've been to, normally it's 40 minutes at the most, but usually 30. There was a lovely big park next to the school so I would take my lunch with me and sit on a bench on my own enjoying the goings on. This was a great way to refresh every day and it was a particularly warm Autumn so I was able to enjoy going there all the time.

The staffroom had a lovely atmosphere with everybody talking to each other, rather than about each other, but for me I just wanted to be outside as much as possible so the park was ideal. I got to chat to the staff for my 15 minute coffee break every morning and they were all very down to earth and friendly, the best so far.

I looked forward to going to school, finally I found one I enjoyed and wanted to be at. What a difference this made to my wellbeing and it was noticed by my family and friends.

I worked with one little girl in Year 1 who was very contrary. She would spend most of the morning asking me, almost pleading, if it it was her turn and I would let her know when it would be, which was usually just before lunch or towards the end of the day. Then when it was her turn to work with me she would hide in the class or run to the area we worked in to sit in my big swivel chair before I could get to it.

As I got to know her I found lots of different activities to do that she enjoyed. I saw a quick improvement in her abilities once I knew what she was capable of and what she needed support with. She liked playing games so I used that as an end reward if she did her interventions first.

By choosing a game to play at the start of our session, so that it was ready, she became very compliant with her actual work and was very precise in what she produced. She was a manipulative and controlling child, but had a sweet side that I was lucky to have seen.

Most of the staff didn't like her and dreaded working with her, but I felt I was getting a lot out of her and we liked each other. I was teaching and she was learning and we were having fun on the way (as long as she won all the games) What more can you ask?

A little boy in Year 1 was an absolute hoot to work with as he came out with all sorts of things, talk about a vivid imagination. He was usually the first child of the day that I would take to my area to work with and Monday mornings were always something to look forward to.

I always ask any children I've ever worked with if they've had a nice weekend or what they've done and this boy had some very tall stories. As I was new and only just getting to know all the children I had no clue about their lives so anything they told me I let them believe that I believed, even though his stories in particular were extremely far fetched.

The very first time I met him he told me that he had been up in the air in his Grandad's Spitfire over the weekend and his Grandad let him fly it for a while. He gave me so much detail to this story that I was almost beginning to think it might be true, but I had been warned by staff that he was a story teller, and a good one at that.

The next weekend he went to London and was driven around in his Uncle's doubledecker bus with just him and a friend. They went all over London and visited many places including the Tower of London, where they went into all the rooms and the dungeons and got chased by ghosts. He described everything like it had actually happened.

Other times he went in a tank that his Grandad had built and he let him drive over a line of cars which was "cool" and another time he jumped out of a plane with a parachute on his own, landed in the sea and swam back to the beach then went and had an ice cream. If he doesn't grow up to be a writer I'll eat my hat.

There were many many of these stories from this little boy and I looked forward to hearing them to see what he was going to come out with next. How we ever got any work done I don't know, but we did and he was very good at everything, when he wanted to be. He liked getting stickers and reward charts so that was his daily goal. He was great fun to work with, entertaining and very likeable. He made the day worthwhile.

Being at this school made me realise and appreciate what a school day should be like. The Head stood for no nonsense and all the children were very well behaved. The staff were all consistent with their managing of the children and their behaviour. At last, this is how it should be.

CHAPTER 21

The one that I remember the most and am most proud of at that school was a little girl in Reception who was a selective mute due to major trauma in her life. I shall refer to her as 'S'. She would talk and play with her friends at playtime and run around the playground with them, but as soon as any adult went near her she would go silent. She wouldn't say a word in class to her teacher. I knew this was going to be a challenge.

I worked with S in a group with 3 other children and we would mainly play learning games which they all wanted to win at. I always mixed up the activities so that there were different things to do, I didn't want them getting bored. They all seemed to enjoy everything I gave them to do, some more than others.

Although S took part in this group she wouldn't speak. Her friends spoke for her if needed. One of them even said to me "She won't speak to you, she only speaks to us" to which I replied with a smile directed at S "I'm sure she can tell me that". S smiled at my comment and looked desperately like she wanted to say something, but didn't, she just chuckled instead.

I discovered that S liked some songs when I started singing in the playground one day and her face lit up. She took me by both hands and swayed to one of the songs I was singing. It was a very special moment and I felt I was getting closer to her. It was the sort of song you could use sign language to so that's what I did and she copied me. It's a popular song by a popular artist and every time I hear it I think of her.

We were into my second week at this school and my fourth time taking this small group, it was a twice a week activity with them. We were playing a game where you had to match a body together with 3 different cards, head, body and legs. Sometimes one of us would put something that clearly didn't match for another child to put right and there was lots of laughter with this game, including S which was lovely to hear.

I was deliberately putting things in the wrong place so that the children would correct me to make them feel good. I put a card down and said it was a blue skirt and then S said as clear as day "That's not a skirt it's a pair of trousers".

Inside I was bursting that she had finally spoken, and so clearly, but I couldn't make a fuss so just said "Oh silly me, you're right" and carried on. We were almost at the end of the game when this happened. S didn't say anything else, but she continued giggling and took charge in clearing away.

We were running late so I told the children they could go as it was lunch time, but she stayed to help me. As we were putting the game away I started singing the song and she joined in, not using sign language but her voice. I couldn't believe it, I was overjoyed.

I virtually skipped down the corridor with her and took her into her class where I told the teacher what had happened (out of S's earshot). She too couldn't believe it. This was the most rewarding day of my career without a doubt.

From then on she became more and more chatty with me. For someone who is a selective mute and so young she was very articulate. I never reacted with any kind of look of surprise when she spoke as I didn't think it would be the right thing to do, but would always just carry on like it was natural.

There was one time when we were in our usual place in our group and, by now, word had got out that S was speaking to me. There was great excitement about this among the staff and they were all keen to hear her.

We were doing our usual thing, one of our interventions that involved a lot of speaking, when two members of staff walked by. They gave me a look as if to say could I get her to talk and they went round the corner towards a classroom, but I could see they were waiting. S couldn't see as she had her back to them so didn't feel intimidated by them being there.

I carried on with the activity directing it at S and she answered quite wordy. These two staff members were beside themselves and struggled to control their disbelief in hearing S talk for the first time.

They composed themselves then walked back again, but S immediately stopped talking in mid flow and followed them with her eyes until they were out of sight then carried on with what she had been saying.

S was producing some lovely work and had the most beautiful handwriting for someone so young. She especially liked colouring in pictures and was always very careful to keep inside the lines. I was getting a lot out of her in our group and she genuinely seemed to enjoy the activities.

When I went into her classroom to gather the children for these sessions she would always be first to come to me and wanted to be first to sit at our table as she had a preferred seat.

She became increasingly confident and this was a wonderful experience to have been a part of. I really felt like I was doing a good job and that all my training and my own life experience was paying off at this school.

For the first time in years I wasn't just following children round or trying to entice them into their classroom or sheltering from flying objects! Here they all wanted to learn and were all a joy to work with.

CHAPTER 22

Even though I was Supply staff I was made to feel part of that school team. I was really enjoying going in every day, not knowing what stories I was going to hear from my little man or what events were going to happen, but this is now March 2020 and we all know what that meant!

I stayed on for the first week that the country shut down as we still had Keyworker children who had to come to school. There were 12 children in total in the whole school and it was a very weird time for all of us. We started every morning with a Joe Wicks workout in the hall to get us ready for the day ahead.

The children thought it was very exciting that they were all together in the same class even though they were different year groups. There was a new way of teaching to cover this, but it worked.

I was just getting used to this new system when I received a letter on the first Friday of that week from the NHS telling me that I was in the 'high risk category' if I got coronavirus due to the medication I was on and that I should stop working immediately. I was devastated that I couldn't return.

Never thought I'd say that before! Infact an excuse like this to stop work at any other school would have been ideal, but not anymore. I had finally found a school that I can honestly say I loved going to and felt properly appreciated and accepted and then this happened. I was happy there, I didn't want to leave, but had no choice. So, like most of the rest of the country, I stayed at home isolating.

Although I was sad to no longer be at this school I was also really enjoying being at home and especially being in my garden. It was an exceptional Spring starting with the warmest, dryest February on record, going into March which was very warm and then having a long, hot Summer with no rain at all until late August.

When it eventually did rain it was very strange. The sky was leaking. What was this wet stuff coming from the clouds? It had been so long which is most unusual for England.

Coronavirus was killing a lot of people and making many extremely ill so it was a truly awful time for the world, but for me it did me the power of good. It made me realise what's important in life and I really started to properly appreciate what I've got.

Nobody could see anybody outside their home for months and everything was closed, apart from food shops, so spending time with family was the only thing we could do.

We spent hours playing board games or pingpong in the most fabulous sunshine and discovering new walks in our area, which I thought we had exhausted by now over the years, but no, we found plenty more. I ended up not working at all for 18 months and enjoyed every moment. I also continued doing the Joe Wicks workouts every morning at home and this made me feel great.

CHAPTER 23

The time had come to think about returning to work. Covid (as it was now being called) was easing and shops and offices were slowly starting to open up again. Part of me felt like I never wanted to work again, but my bank balance was telling me something different!

The agency offered me an ongoing role in two different year groups. Year 3 in the morning with two boys who had limited English and Year 5 in the afternoon with a boy who was undiagnosed, but definitely had needs. This was a school I had been to before, the one where the Head Teacher had come to introduce herself to me, but I knew she was no longer there and it was now a new Head.

I thought this would be a really nice, varied job, mixing it up by working with different year groups. Both teachers were really nice to work with and had so much patience. I felt I fitted in quite quickly and got to know the children that needed more attention almost immediately.

I had a nice first morning with my Year 3 boys who were both very quiet and willing to learn. Not such a good start for Year 5 though. When I entered the room they were in the middle of a lesson, but one child was outside banging his head on the window, another child was under a table refusing to come out, two children were wandering around aimlessly with no interest or intention of doing any work, another was outside on the trim trail and another was shouting and swearing in the corridor. "Welcome to Year 5" the class teacher said to me. These particular children were all boys.

All the other children in the class were getting on with their work and taking no notice of what was going on like it was an every day occurance, which I soon discovered it was. This class was crazy! If it hadn't been so shocking, it would have been comical, but it really wasn't. This was going to be my afternoons from here on.

The boy I was on a 1-2-1 with was actually in the class at his desk with his work book open. The timing wasn't great as I was having my lunch for the first half an hour of their lesson so I was missing what they were supposed to be doing.

I was introduced to him and sat down with him, asking him what he was doing and he seemed very compliant, something I hadn't expected when staff knew it was him I would be working with and what they had told me.

I expected some sort of demon child, but this boy was sweet and willing to work - at first. He wrote the date and a few lines. I did notice how bad his writing was for a year 5 child, especially compared to most of the others, but I soon realised that he hardly writes anything at all and this was him making a good impression on my first visit.

I concentrated solely on working with him (let's called him K), but the behaviour of at least five other boys in that class overshadowed everything. They were unbelievably rude and non-compliant. The teacher apologised to me and said "I just don't know what to do with them, they never listen and do what they like, we can't force them to sit and learn".

She was an extremely calm and likeable lady, but every now and then would need to use her 'big voice' just to be heard over their nonsense. I admired her patience, but felt so sorry for her having to be with these particular children all day every day. The short time I was there was bad enough, I couldn't imagine what it must be like all the time!

One of them did everything he could to be outside, often just getting up and leaving the room without asking. Another made a silly baby noise when you tried to talk to him, like a squeaky toy almost. He wasn't the only one in that class to make these noises and that made it difficult, and annoying, to talk to them or help them.

They could all talk perfectly well, but chose to act like babies! One minute they're walking around thinking that they're big and tough, the next they're squeaking at us. This was going to be a difficult class to manage I can see.

Another boy was often angry and became like the Incredible Hulk when things didn't go his way. He liked fighting and swearing and this was very scary at times. For the first few days I thought that K was a wonderful child to support, compared to those other boys, but by the end of the week, out he came.

He began to say "No" when I asked him to do things and all he wanted to do was be on the Chromebook. The teacher allowed him to do this to keep him happy, so long as he was doing things he should be doing and nothing else.

He really liked music so always went to YouTube first to pick something to listen to as background while "working". Usually it was music from a game. He was very big into Gaming and several of them would talk about different games they had played the night before, either on their own or with each other online. It was a whole new language for me, I had no idea what they were going on about.

I found myself often struggling to get their attention because they were so focussed on talking about Gaming and games. I tended to take K out of the classroom and into the corridor where there was a table for him to work at as he seemed happier there than in the class and the teacher encouraged this. It was easier for her if he was out of the room.

The trouble with that was the other children would come out to see what he was doing so would leave their own work. I was in a no win situation. Despite the teacher telling them to go back into the classroom, they would ignore her and carry on talking about Gaming with K.

As we can't physically pick these children up and carry them back to class we could only do our best to guide them back or threaten them with a visit from the Head, but that had no impact whatsoever.

There was a small room supervised by two lovely SEN leaders and every day these children would end up being taken to this room to calm down. I actually think they played up so that they could go to this room as they were given different things to do and they avoided their learning with the rest of the class.

K couldn't be in the class as he was too disruptive. He would always call out instead of putting his hand up and would often go right up to the teacher and tap her for attention. This made it very difficult for her to do her job so that's why he spent alot of time in the corridor. It was his choice though.

If he could behave he could be in class with his friends, but he couldn't control himself which made it unfair on everyone else. He was an extremely demanding boy who liked the word "No". The more he got to know me, the more I would see what I had been warned about from other staff members.

He was sent home a couple of times during my time with him for extremely bad behaviour, but he told me he plays on his Xbox and so likes being 'excluded' from school.

He had also started making those silly baby noises which just made the whole thing impossible. Everytime I spoke to him he would squeak at me or shout "No". I was only in Year 5 for an hour and a half every day, but my goodness it seemed like an eternity with the constant bad behaviour and defiance from them.

I looked forward to my Year 3 start every day, but even that was becoming increasingly difficult. There were two boys in there who had issues and made the classroom an uncomfortable place to be in at times. I was happy to take my two out of the class to work in the Library where we had peace and quiet, away from the drama.

Most mornings there would be a problem of some sorts with either or both of these boys. One was a very angry little boy and the other would copy him, so both would be angry and, dare I say, nasty little boys?

The class teacher cried on my shoulder a couple of times I was at this school and actually ended up leaving at the same time as I did, along with another qualified teacher and several TA's. They had just had enough of all the nonsense and bad leadership from the new Head, who had absolutely no control whatsoever.

I tried really hard to stick it out. I was supposed to be there for a whole school year, but after one term I was done, and even that was too long. It was awful and a school I will not go back to. K went from bad to worse.

I went in bright and breezy one afternoon and the first thing he did was make a sick sort of noise at me and stuck out his tongue. I said "Oh charming" and the teacher said he had been doing it all day and it was driving her mad. She was glad to see me so I could take him out of class.

I couldn't speak to him at all without him making this new horrible noise which seemed to be infectious as three of the other boys also started doing it!!! This is not how I want to spend my days, I'm out of here. I held on until the end of term, as I knew they were struggling for staff, and then I was gone.

To be fair to the class teacher all the children in her class (apart from the five I've mentioned) were lovely, well mannered, polite, wanting to learn and would ignore everything going on around them.

This, of course, irritated the ones who wanted attention, but they've all been together in this class since Year 1 so have grown up with each other and know how each other behave and misbehave. They were a credit to the teacher who I felt really sorry to be leaving behind as we got on really well. I hope things have improved, but somehow I just can't see it.

What is going on in schools? When did children start to think it was ok to be so rude and do what they like? I think every day should begin with a 20 minute lesson in general manners and respect. It seems like a lot of children play up so they can be sent home, which is exactly what they want.

So many have said to me that when they go home they play on their XBox, that's their punishment for their bad behaviour at school! It's probably easier for their parents too.

Lots of schools give children three chances to improve and if they've had to be spoken to and their parents called in a third time they then get sent home. These children are controlling and manipulative.

I have noticed in shops how young people are towards customers. Back in the day staff always used to make polite conversation and would do as much as they could to help. Now you're lucky if you can find anyone to help and, if you can, they're as miserable as sin and make you feel like you're a nuisance.

Very few have any general knowledge of what's in the shop they work in and have to refer to their phones. I do worry what the world is going to be like in 20 or even 10 years time with the generation that is coming up. It is, of course, not all of them, but God help us all.

CHAPTER 24

I felt a huge weight off my shoulders having finished at that school and now it was Christmas and we could celebrate with family and friends once again. I was really unsure and apprehensive about starting work again, but knew I needed to.

Incase you're wondering why I continue to work in education after all the stories I've told and complaining that I've done, I have, over the years, looked for other lines of work, but nothing comes close. The hours are the best part of it and the school holidays, of which there are many.

There are very few, if any, other jobs which offer anything like school hours and it suits me down to the ground. Home by 3.30pm most of the time (when not in a nursery) and lots of holidays throughout the year. Any other jobs I've looked at involve working weekends or late into the evening, no thank you, not at my age now anyway. Aswell as all that there would undoubtedly be lots of training and I definitely feel beyond that now.

I anxiously waited for the agency to contact me with a job offer and had already told them I didn't want to be too far from home. I had considered going back to day to day work, but with Covid still rife it was a much wiser decision to stick to the same school.

I had already decided that I only wanted to work four days a week, having Fridays off as I need to start slowing down with my work hours I feel. My son doesn't work on a Friday either so we quite often do things together which I look forward to and enjoy with him.

The agency offered me another local school, one that I had only been to for one day a few years ago. It's reputation was good and I know there are staff there who have been there for years, which is often a good sign.

The boy I would be supporting was in Year 1, yet undiagnosed, but clearly has needs of sorts. He's the type of child that likes to hide, says "NO" alot and doesn't think anything of blowing a raspberry in your face!

It was the first day of a new term year. When I entered the classroom I couldn't distinguish between him and the rest of the children as he was sat still with the others and nothing was standing out that I could spot him. With everything I had been told about him I expected him to be off and running. He played nicely all day and appeared to do all that was asked of him.

The next day his true colours came out. He wouldn't come into the classroom and just kept screeching and blowing raspberries at me, which is one thing I can't stand, it's SO disgusting!

The class teacher was lovely, extremely calm and patient. He eventually responded to her, but after much persuasion. I knew I had my work cut out with this one. I soon realised that he was the best of the bunch as there were two other Year 1 classes with at least 6 other boys who showed outrageous behaviour.

Considering how young they were they really didn't seem to care how they spoke to an adult or how they behaved. This included refusing to come in from playtime and staff having to radio for help, kicking doors and walls, screaming the place down for hours, spitting at staff and generally being really unkind to us all, and not doing any or little work.

Despite all this bad behaviour we would have to remain calm and try talking them round. This school offers lots of praise and stickers for the tiniest positive thing these children do, but very little consequences for the way they carry on. I felt like I was constantly negotiating with these children.

One of these boys was very rude to me during a group activity and blew a raspberry right in my face. A teacher saw this and told him to apologise, but he got up and ran off. I followed after him and managed to bring him back to the group. He sat still for 1 minute and got the thumbs up from the teacher who then gave him a sticker and said "Good boy, you're doing really good sitting and listening".

Surely this is offering mixed messages? Barely anything for being that way towards me, but a sticker and a thumbs up for sitting still for a minute! I couldn't quite believe it, but I saw it all the time at this school.

Some children go home with lots of stickers on their jumpers and when the parents ask what sort of a day they've had the teacher tells them a good one. What about all the bad stuff they've done during the day, upsetting staff and damaging school equipment? Does that get mentioned? No, or rarely anyway.

Most of these children have a 1-2-1, but even then they still do whatever they like. I can understand why the school want to promote all the positive behaviour, but something must be done about the negative, of which goes on all day long from these boys. It's draining and wrong. All we're asked to do is write up what we witness so that it builds up a complete picture of the child's behaviour for possible future exclusion or suspension.

I was asked to sit with one of these boys in the afternoon and to make sure he did his work away from his class and the other children. It was only when the day was nearly over that I found out why this was happening. He had hurt a teacher so much that she had to go home in severe pain. Why did it take so long for me to be told of something so serious? They told me I was an invaluable part of the team and how well they thought I was doing, and yet I was told nothing about something like this, it made no sense.

The longer I was at this school the more I realised that I was in the best class by far compared to the others. The boy I was supporting started to respond well to me and did the work expected of him in class with either me or the teacher. He tried hard to ignore the behaviour of the others that was always going on outside our door and made a huge improvement in his behaviour over time.

I think there must be someone up there in the higher authorities that is suggesting this positive approach as it seems to be going on in a lot of schools now. I'm all for this, but PLEASE don't keep ignoring the truly awful behaviour as it's not fair on them, other children and staff. Yes it's more understandable if the child has a condition, but from what I have seen over the years so much of it is just really extreme bad behaviour!

How will these children ever learn if they keep being rewarded for the smallest good thing they do, but so little gets done about their bad behaviour? Internal exclusion must be the answer, so long as they are actually doing school work and not just playing games or on the Chromebook as these are rewards. I didn't stay at this school for any longer than originally planned even though they asked me to stay on for another term.

CHAPTER 25

Time for a break from that school. Fortunately, and to my delight, the agency offered me a role in a local school that I had been to before and had enjoyed my short time there. I would be working on a 1-2-1 with a Year 2 boy (they like giving me the boys) who was behind with the curriculum, had no behaviour issues and just needed extra support.

On my first day there he wasn't in for register. This was unusal apparently and I thought it wasn't a good start, but then I heard crying in the corridor and a bit of commotion. I had a feeling that this was going to be my boy and instantly felt anxious that perhaps this was going to be more difficult than I had anticipated.

He was coaxed away from his mum by a teacher familiar to him and taken into class. I was told that this was a boy who had a routine of coming in to school early and did not like being late and last. He was a really sweet little boy, fairly quiet, but very likeable and compliant. He did like to sit on the carpet with his friends for learning time, but when it came to then doing the work I would either take him out of the room where we would work together or take a small group or work in the classroom. This suited him, me and the class teacher so we were all happy.

When I first met him he could write some letters, but couldn't say what they were. Apart from his name, which he wrote backwards, he couldn't form any words. He seemed to like writing random letters so my job was to help him recognise them and put them together to make words. At first it was like every Monday we would have to start all over again as he had forgotten everything he learnt the week before, but then all of a sudden he was remembering things and telling me what the letters were.

Initially I had to write a letter for him to copy, but then he grasped what they were, so if I said to write 'p' or 'a' or any other letter of the alphabet he was finally able to do it without having to copy. Everything started off back to front, including his numbers, but now he thinks before he writes anything and, more often than not, gets it the right way round and can tell me what it is. Now we just need to start putting them together to make words. He loves me reading stories to him and my goal is for him to one day read a story to me, maybe even one of my own stories.

Inbetween my work as a TA I spent time writing children's rhyming stories, both of which have been published so I am also an Author. I take every opportunity I can to let schools that I work in know this and I often read to individual classes and take questions. That in itself is extremely satisfying, having a class of children gazing up at you while you read your own story to them and then ask questions as they're genuinly interested and so many will say that they want to write books and become Authors when they grow up.

It's moments like that that make the job worthwhile and rewarding. I instantly knew I was going to be happy in this role as I was being listened to and I was supporting a lovely little boy who wanted to learn, hoorah. The other children in the class were all really nice too, with the exception of one or two, but that seems to come as standard everywhere.

We were all on the carpet having a group discussion and the teacher asked them if they could remember an item that had been used in the story she had just read them. She was giving them a clue by using the national hand gesture for a camera, but they all looked blankly at her.

She had to tell them what it was then one child said quietly "That's a funny camera". I guess this generation only really use their phones to take photos so that's why they didn't recognise the gesture. It's such a fast changing world that you have to think about everything you do otherwise children will pick up on it.

Even the gesture for using a phone has changed to a flat hand to the ear as opposed to a fist to the ear and dialling with the index finger. They wouldn't have a clue what that was now.

Before I started at this school I had thought about finishing for the Easter holidays and not returning to work until September, having that whole period off to myself, but I have enjoyed it so much that I plan to be there until the end of the Summer Term, much to the school's delight.

I have finally found a school that I am truly happy in. The staff are all friendly, most of the children are lovely and my training and experiences over the years are paying off. I feel included, supported, accepted and appreciated. Only one other school has made me feel this way and at this stage I have been to so many I've lost count. Many of which I haven't even had any tales to tell about so are not covered.

It's taken 7 years to get here, but I am at last happy at school. My depression is dwindling and my anxiety levels are nowhere near as high as they have been in the past. I'm still suffering with the menopause, but surely to God that's coming to an end soon, it's now almost 10 years!

Some readers will view this book as incredibly negative, that I'm being harsh towards schools, nurseries and staff and unsympathetic towards the children I have talked about. Believe me, in our job as a TA we have to show complete sympathy, choose our wording very carefully and have the patience of a saint. We are actors during the day on a TA salary.

Teachers, TA's, Support Staff and anyone else who has worked in schools will be able to relate to most of my stories and perhaps even recognise the situations. I don't know what goes on anywhere else, but these are my experiences in my area.

Something I would love to do is visit different schools across the country and even the world to see how it is and what goes on. It can't just be this small part of England that we wrap our children up so much in cottonwool that they feel they can get away with anything?

If teachers and TA's don't already do this I think it would be beneficial to visit as many other schools as possible too. So many that I've met over the years have only been to the one school they are currently working in and so have nothing to compare it to.

There is really good management out there and it shows instantly with the atmosphere, the behaviour of the children and the happiness in the staff. If only all schools could have those qualities and whatever training those headteachers are given. Shouldn't we all be operating the same way with the same rules, consequences and rewards?

I wanted to end on a happy note after all the negativity that I've written about. Reading back on it I sound like a right old Moaning Minnie (as my Nana used to say), but I'm really not. Maybe my next book, covering the next 7 years of working as a TA will be more joyous and comical as I'm now in a more positive state of mind? I will by then be reaching my retirement so my job as a TA will soon become a distant memory, or will it?

Ingram Content Group UK Ltd.
Milton Keynes UK
UKHW010852100323
418370UK00004B/404